Growing Through God's Word

Janis Cox

Growing Through God's Word
Copyright © 2020 by Janis Cox

All rights reserved. No part of this publication may be reproduced, distributed or transmitted in any form or by any means, including photocopying, recording, or other electronic or mechanical methods, without the prior written permission of the publisher, except in the case of brief quotations embodied in critical reviews and certain other non-commercial uses permitted by copyright law. For permission requests, write to the publisher, addressed "Attention: Permissions Coordinator," at the address below.

All Scripture quotations, unless otherwise indicated, are taken from the Holy Bible, New International Version®, NIV®. Copyright ©1973, 1978, 1984, 2011 by Biblica, Inc.™ Used by permission of Zondervan. All rights reserved worldwide. www.zondervan.com The "NIV" and "New International Version" are trademarks registered in the United States Patent and Trademark Office by Biblica, Inc.™

Scripture quotations marked MSG are taken from THE MESSAGE, copyright © 1993, 2002, 2018 by Eugene H. Peterson. Used by permission of NavPress. All rights reserved. Represented by Tyndale House Publishers, a Division of Tyndale House Ministries.

Scripture taken from the NKJV New King James Version®. Copyright © 1982 by Thomas Nelson. Used by permission. All rights reserved.

Scripture quotations are from the ESV® Bible (The Holy Bible, English Standard Version®), copyright © 2001 by Crossway Bibles, a publishing ministry of Good News Publishers. Used by permission. All rights reserved.

Scripture quotations marked (NLT) are taken from the Holy Bible, New Living Translation, copyright ©1996, 2004, 2015 by Tyndale House Foundation. Used by permission of Tyndale House Publishers, Inc., Carol Stream, Illinois 60188. All rights reserved.

Scripture taken from the NEW AMERICAN STANDARD BIBLE(R), Copyright ©1960,1962,1963,1968,1971,1972,1973,1975,1977,1995 by The Lockman Foundation. Used by permission.

All artwork produced by Janis Cox. All scripture unless noted is from NIV.

Published by Butterfly Beacons www.janiscox.com

Library and Archives Canada Cataloguing in Publication
Cox, Janis, 1949
    Growing Through God's Word/Janis Cox

ISBN 978-1-9995438-5-3 (paperback)
    1. Titl

Endorsements

"Janis Cox is a prayer warrior with a passion for helping others find their way closer to God through His Word. With short devotions, heartfelt original prayers and tips for ways to pray, Growing Through God's Word provides soul-nourishing morsels for those hungry to grow their faith and see God at work in their lives."

~ JANINE UNGVARSKY, LAY MINISTER/WRITER

"We say "Speak Lord. I hear you; but God says, "Child, are you really listening?" Experience really listening with a gentle nudge from this book."

~ BRENDA J WOOD, PROLIFIC AUTHOR, MOTIVATIONAL SPEAKER. LATEST BOOK … *How to Live Like a Princes*s (when your life is the pits!)

"Growing Through God's Word is a treasure, filled with practical steps you can take to build your personal relationship with God, through Bible reading and prayer. The book points us towards pitfalls that we may encounter and ways to open yourself to God's will."

~ CARMEN NULAND, FOLLOWER OF JESUS

"Personal anecdotes on the topic, backed by Scripture verses, illustrations from the author's own Bible, challenges, and questions to think about involve the reader on many levels. I believe these short study topics can be returned to time and again to gain more insight into our walk with God. I appreciated the resources listed at the end to enable me to go deeper into the topics to grow deeper in my relationship with God. Jan adds a personal touch by offering to pray for us, the readers, at the end of each section. A book I would recommend having and using for personal Bible study and reflection."

~ CAROL HARRISON, INSPIRATIONAL SPEAKER, PUBLISHED AUTHOR AND STORYTELLER

"I love this book. Jan shares personal insights and stories straight from the heart. I also love that she uses a lot of scripture. This book is Refreshing! Hopeful! Guiding us in our walk with the Lord!"

~JOLENA AKERS WELKER, RETIRED LIBRARIAN, BIBLE STUDY LEADER

"Who wouldn't want their faith to grow as big as a sequoia tree? In Janis Cox's book, Growing Through God's Word, I find scriptures that inspire me to pray daily and practical tips for growing my faith, such as her ~ "How to Be a Better Prayer: Ten Simple Ideas".
Thank you, Janis Cox, for writing this devotional book. It helps me spend more quality time reading God's Word, praying, and listening for what He wants me to hear."

~ KARYN ALMENDAREZ, AUTHOR OF *Tragedy's Treasures, a Mom Finds Hope in Grief and Loss*

Dedication

My Bible sat on my shelf for years. Occasionally I would take it out and look for crossword puzzle answers. When my youngest was born, I read the Psalms. They comforted me as I struggled to regain energy. But the rest of the time, my Bible sat – neglected.

Penny entered my life in 1999. The new church we attended offered a course called *The Workbook of Living Prayer*, by Maxi Dunham. The leader was Penny. I had never met her but felt courageous one Sunday morning to approach her and ask her if she thought I could join.

I explained my lack of Bible experience. With the warmest smile, she assured me that this course would not only open the doors to reading the Bible but also learning to pray. I took the plunge and life has never been the same.

Thank you, Penny, for all you do in teaching others to follow Jesus.

Foreword

I truly can't remember when my path crossed with that of Janis'. It's no more than a couple of years ago and yet, it feels as if I've known her forever. I told her we are PIAP's. Peas in a Pod. The way we think and feel and how spontaneously we interact.

There's no great secret there. She's a Woman of God and it shows in so many ways. She's helpful, far beyond what is required. She's humble. I doubt if she realizes how talented she is. In her art. In her writing. I adore the little prayers requests interspersed throughout Growing Through God's Word.

The first one in her book:

"May I pray for you and me?

Lord Jesus, You came to earth to show us the way. You came to teach us about God. You talked about who God is and You showed miracles about how big our God is. Please help us to have that mustard seed of faith to put our trust in You. In Jesus' name. Amen.

Think about your prayer time. Are you spending time in prayer and reading God's Word?"

And that sets the tone for this amazing little gem. This book is a keeper; hence I'm holding out for the print version.

She made a list of ten ideas which inspired her in her prayer life.

The one that grabbed me:

"Journal your prayers and listen for God-ideas."

Bijoux abound but another that got my attention:

"Find a quiet spot and pray. Then listen to what God has to say. If you don't wake early enough, ask God to wake you up. Be refreshed and ready to come to Him and be restored. Read His Word and grow."

Janis is an early riser. She doesn't need an alarm. God wakes her because He's waiting. And those precious morning hours are gold. As another early riser I know I can reach out to Jan as she will be awake and in God's company.

There's more in this book than can be absorbed in one read through. There are small treasures to discover on every page. I know I have to go back and do a ton more concentrated reading.

But always, always that lovely refrain from time to time:

May I pray for you and me?

Yes, Janis. Please do.

~ Ida Adams - Writer/Dreamer. Not of this world. Just passing through. Lover of All Creatures Great and Small. Unapologetic Christian.

Introduction

Twenty years ago, I felt lost. I had a loving family. Everyone was well. Our business grew. But I had a burning question, "What is life? What am I here for?"

I grew up in a church, knew some Bible stories, but somehow missed the "who is Jesus" answer. I didn't understand creation or God's plan for the world.

God opened the door.

He knew I struggled to find Him. In 1999, with a friend of my daughter's, we all attended an Easter Service at a contemporary church in a neighbouring city. This church resonated with music and testimonies. My heart fluttered as a little dryness fell away.

I didn't know of a similar church nearby. Could I find one? The answer – yes. God led me through a new friend to a faith-filled church in our area. The church belonged to the same group of churches I had attended previously.

I started to go to their services. God opened my eyes and I grew to know Him. But I still questioned, "Who is this Jesus?" I read Christian books and began to believe as I attended Bible studies. I questioned.

God answered.

My Bible sat on the shelf. I didn't think I could understand it. Encouraged by my friend Penny (see my Dedication page), I started my journey to know God through His Word.

I picked up that book, the Bible. I read it. I studied it. I memorized it.

I even painted it as I started to do Bible art.

God "spoke" to me for the first time at a Christian retreat when I read the following:

> *"When they had finished eating, Jesus said to Simon Peter, 'Simon son of John, do you love me more than these?' 'Yes, Lord,' he said, 'you know that I love you.' Jesus said, 'Feed my lambs.'"* (John 21:15, NIV)

If I loved God, I needed to use my gift of writing to feed others.

That's been my goal.

The following devotionals came from studying His Word. They were first aired on *HopeStreamRadio* an Internet Christian radio station. Thank you, Ron Hughes, for teaching and coaching me in that new endeavour.

Thank you to my loving husband who supports me all the time. Thanks to Snowball, our little Maltipoo, who keeps me company while I write.

Thanks to a group of online friends who became a support team to fine-tune this work. I appreciate every one of you.

Thanks to the friends at Wellington Square and Haliburton United who continued to encourage me on my walk with God. A special thanks to Donna who not only prayed for me but encouraged me to come to her church. We have moved to a new area and I am praying for that encouragement to continue.

May you, the reader, open your mind, heart and soul to listen to what God says through His Word. I encourage you to keep your journal handy to share your thoughts and reflections.

I believe my purpose is to spread the love of Jesus and to help people grow by reading His Word.

> *"They're holding on, not because of what they think they're going to get out of it, but because they're convinced of God's grace and purpose in choosing them. If they were only thinking of their immediate self-interest, they would have left long ago." (Romans 11:6, MSG)*

May I pray for you and me?

Lord Jesus, open the eyes of each person who opens Your Word. Teach us all the way to read, study and listen to You. Please help us to make the time because we know we can't do this life alone. In Jesus' name. Amen

ENDORSEMENTS 3

DEDICATION 6

FOREWORD 7

INTRODUCTION 10

WHAT CAN WE LEARN FROM A TINY SEED? 19

HOW TO BE A BETTER PRAY-ER: TEN SIMPLE IDEAS 24

HOW TO REGENERATE GOD'S POWER IN YOUR LIFE 29

HOW CAN I BE RESTORED, HEALED AND FIND PEACE? 35

DOES GOD REALLY WANT TO MEET WITH ME? 41

HOW NOT TO BE HELD CAPTIVE BY FEAR 47

CAN YOU FOLLOW THE HOLY SPIRIT? 54

WHO ME? DENY MYSELF?......................58

HOW TO LIVE VICARIOUSLY THROUGH CHRIST
..................63

ASK A FORTUNE TELLER? 68

WHY ARE YOU POISONING YOURSELF? 73

HOW AND WHY I SHOULD STOP SAYING THE "S" WORD..................80

WHAT HAPPENS WHEN THE FIRE ALARM IS PULLED? 85

TRAVEL TO THE END OF THE KNOWN UNIVERSE AND WHAT IS FOUND? 91

WHAT MADE MY HUSBAND MUTTER, "YES, DEAR", ALL THE TIME?..................95

HOW A HEARING LOSS TAUGHT ME TO LISTEN TO GOD 99

IT'S HARD TO STOP THE MENTAL RACKET WHEN I PRAY 104

FIVE WAYS TO LEARN HOW TO DEVOTE YOURSELF TO PRAYER 108

HOW OUR AMAZING GOD CHANGES OUR NEWNESS 113

WHAT'S UNDER THERE? 118

PRAYER BOOKS 122

DEVOTIONAL/TEACHING BOOKS/RESOURCES 122

ABOUT THE AUTHOR 123

What Can We Learn from a Tiny Seed?

Matthew 17:20

> *He replied, "Because you have so little faith. Truly I tell you, if you have faith as small as a mustard seed, you can say to this mountain, 'Move from here to there,' and it will move. Nothing will be impossible for you."*

Did you know that from one of the smallest seeds grows one of the largest trees?

The seed of the sequoia is only ¼ the size of a grain of uncooked rice. And yet it grows into the biggest tree, having roots that can cover over between two and four acres and bark that can be two feet thick.

I find that amazing!

And can you imagine our earth without seeds? There would be very little plant growth.

In **Genesis 1:11-13,**

> *God spoke: "Earth, green up! Grow all varieties of seed-bearing plants,*

> *Every sort of fruit-bearing tree.*
> *And there it was.*
>
> *Earth produced green seed-bearing plants,*
> *all varieties,*
>
> *And fruit-bearing trees of all sorts.*
> *God saw that it was good.*
>
> *It was evening, it was morning—*
> *Day Three. (MSG)*

Jesus told this parable: From **Matthew 13:31-32**

> *"The kingdom of heaven is like a mustard seed, which a man took and planted in his field. Though it is the smallest of all seeds, yet when it grows, it is the largest of garden plants and becomes a tree, so that the birds come and perch in its branches."*

Have you looked at a seed lately?

As I planted my garden this spring, I marveled that the tiny beet seed would produce luscious red beets; and tomato seeds would grow into tall tomato plants.

But the parable of the tiny mustard seed – that makes more sense when I understand the miracle of a tiny seed growing into a large plant. And that our faith can be like that – small, unassuming, but powerful because we enlist the aid of God.

Mark Batterson in his book study called *Draw the Circle – The 40 Day Prayer Challenge*, reminds us of the miracle of that tiny seed and also how we need to go slow and wait expectantly for our prayers to be answered.

He says:

> *Each prayer is like a seed that gets planted in the ground. It disappears for a season, but it eventually bears fruit that blesses future generations. In fact, our prayers bear fruit forever.* [i]

In this world, we want quick fixes and instant solutions.

Mark says:

> *We want God to microwave solutions, MapQuest directions and Twitter instructions.* [ii]

We forget; yes, we forget that we serve a powerful awesome God.

In **Psalm 50** we hear that God owns the cattle on a thousand hills.

> *for every animal of the forest is mine, and the cattle on a thousand hills. (Psalm 50:10)*

We need to remember that we can't let fear dictate our decisions.

Mark Batterson also says:

> *When Jesus walked out of the tomb, the word impossible was removed from our vocabulary.* [iii]

Our God, who can make a humungous tree grow from a tiny seed, can surely answer our prayers.

Is your God big enough to answer your prayers?
Remember you need to ask.
Dream big and ask our awesome God.

May I pray for you and me?

Lord Jesus, You came to earth to show us the way. You came to teach us about God. You talked about who God is and You showed miracles about how big our God is. Please help us to have that mustard seed of faith to put our trust in You. In Jesus' name. Amen.

Think about your prayer time.
Are you spending time in prayer and reading God's Word?

Journal Your Thoughts

How to Be a Better Pray-er: Ten Simple Ideas

As I progress through the study called *Draw a Circle – A 40 Day Prayer Challenge* by Mark Batterson, I realize how much I still need to learn.

In the past I have read books on prayer such as *Too Busy Not to Pray* by Bill Hybels; *The Workbook of Living Prayer* by Maxi Dunham; all the *Power of Prayer* books by Stormie Omartian and *Why Pray for your Pastor* by Richard Ciaramitaro. And many more.

This time, I decided to post a daily report about each chapter on a Facebook group called *Growing Through God's Word*. This is taking a considerable amount of discipline. Each day I read a chapter, highlighting ideas that resonate with me. Then I write the post. Next, I pray about the Scripture and draw a picture in my Bible to go with the lesson.

While doing this I made a list of ten ideas from the first ten days. I hope some of these inspire you to try to experiment more with prayer.

These are in no particular order.

Pray regularly

The other day I thought of how my connection with God has strengthened in this study. I talk to Him about lots of things and feel a calmness that is certainly supernatural.

Watch for divine appointments

I used to go through my day and just go from one thing to the next. Now I stop and think about what is going on around me. For instance, I remember when I hear an ambulance siren to pray for all concerned.

Obey the prompting of the Holy Spirit

Oh, He has nudged me many times. And if I respond the outcome is miraculous. If I don't respond that opportunity is missed.

Pray "get me through" prayers

Sometimes we need to pray this type of prayer. The circumstances don't change but God is still there if we pray through.

Journal your prayers

These become genesis prayers (prayers that I can see the results when I look back in my journals) and ones that God continues to hear. I love journaling my prayers. I find that writing out my thoughts to God helps me see clearly whether I need to change my thinking and how I could be part of the solution.

Be bold and audacious

I remember painting a lion – reminding me to be as bold as a lion. God is the God of miracles. So ask Him for the impossible.

Act as if God will answer

Believe. Sometimes this is very hard to do when things don't seem to be changing at all. But if we believe He will send rain – then we need to wear hip waders; if we believe he will sell a home, we need to start to clear out stuff. Prepare for the answer.

Listen for God-ideas

"Praystorm". God will give us wonderful ideas. God will show us inspiration where we didn't have it before. By finding the quiet and focusing on listening to Him, we can be filled with His ideas.

Dream big with those God-ideas

I love to dream. I love to imagine doing something, seeing something, being part of something BIG. The dream becomes part of me and my prayers. God becomes active in those prayers.

Pray with audacity and tenacity

Never give up praying. When you least expect it, God comes through. But we have to keep on praying.

I love seeing what God is doing in my life and in the world around me. I love praying.

Will you join me? Find a book on prayer. Read Scriptures on prayer. Pray those Scriptures. Learn more.

May I pray for you and me?

Lord, thank You for this method of communication. Thank You for opening the door to You through Your Son Jesus. Teach us more. Help us to be prayer warriors for Your glory. In Jesus' name. Amen.

Let's ramp up our prayer lives. Let's get closer to the One Who can do the impossible. Read God's Word and grow spiritually.

Journal Your Thoughts

How to Regenerate God's Power in Your Life

We have a water softener in our winter vacation residence in Arizona because the water is extremely hard. I found my hair didn't feel as clean as it did with well water back in our Canadian home.

Water softeners work by using resins to soften the water.

After a while, the resin beads get coated with hard minerals and need to be cleaned. This is called regeneration. A button is pushed on the water softener and the resin is flooded with the brine water cleaning the hardness and sending the residue down the drain.

I liked that picture in a spiritual sense.

I thought of myself as the water softener – my body or "the flesh" as the Bible calls it. I know my flesh can get stale, crusty and hardened because of sin. Sometimes these are sins I don't even recognize.

I need a water softener (Jesus) to be constantly keeping my flesh clean. But I also need a regenerator system to flush out the stuff that sticks to my insides.

A sermon helped me see how this is possible.

Our pastor focused on **Galatians 5:16-25**.

> *So, I say, walk by the Spirit, and you will not gratify the desires of the flesh. For the flesh desires what is contrary to the Spirit, and the Spirit what is contrary to the flesh. They are in conflict with each other so that you are not to do whatever you want.*

So how do I do this if my flesh is so strong?

I want to walk in the power of the Spirit. Don't you?

But how?

Galatians 5:22-23 explains the outcome of walking in the spirit – Fruit.

> *But the fruit of the Spirit is love, joy, peace, patience, kindness, goodness, faithfulness, gentleness, self-control.*

And verse **25**

> *If we live by the Spirit, let us also keep in step with the Spirit.*

All right, I want to do this. I want to walk in the Spirit, keep step in the Spirit.

But HOW?

I think there are 3 essential ways that I can keep in step with the Spirit and keep the power of the Spirit flowing through me.
Read God's Word daily

Daily reading of God's Word is essential for anyone who wants to get closer to God. His Word is truth. This is where we get our nourishment. It is where God speaks to us. We need to establish a daily routine to read at least one verse per day.

There are many ways to do this. Some people read a devotional that has scripture over which to ponder. Others may read chapters and settle on something that God has pointed to.

I have a method called the SIMPLE method of studying the Bible, where I can search one verse, study it in context and then listen to what God is saying. And I want to memorize it too. I find art helps me do this, too.

Prayer

Yes, we need to talk to God. I always pray before, during and after I study God's Word. And throughout the day as well. I want to stay close to the One who gives me life. He speaks when I listen. I must communicate with Him.

Clean out the gunk

This is what I realized recently. I have to clean out my system. Routinely. Yes, I need to regenerate. Even with regular Bible study and prayer, my soul can get hardened. I can let unfruitful fleshy things infest my soul.

I need to push that REGENERATE button.

How can I do that?

In private I can confess my sins to God and receive His forgiveness.

But a more powerful way is to partake of Holy Communion with a group of like-minded believers. This can cleanse me of all sin (even those hidden ones) and God's mercy flows during the taking of the bread and the wine.

During communion, I can feel the flow of His forgiveness when I take the bread and the wine. He flushes me clean. Inspires me anew to write for His glory.

Just as the old hymn says:

What can wash away my sin?
Nothing but the blood of Jesus. (Public Domain)

Now I am renewed, reinvigorated, and regenerated. I am filled with the power of the Holy Spirit, ready to do His will.

May I pray for you and me?

Lord, we love that you want this close relationship with us. We want to get closer and closer to you. We know you have set up the means for us to do that – through your Word, Prayer and Communion. Thank You so much. Help us to grow and produce much fruit to glorify Your Name. Thank You, Jesus. Amen.

Are you using the three methods of producing spiritual fruit? Learn to hear God's Word through scripture and prayer and be cleansed by His blood through confession and taking of the elements in communion.

Journal Your Thoughts

How Can I Be Restored, Healed and Find Peace?

Restore

This, to me, is the most important word in our Christian Faith.

Reading in Psalm 23 from the (NKJV):

> *The Lord is my shepherd;*
>
> *I shall not want.*
>
> *He makes me to lie down in green pastures;*
>
> *He leads me beside the still waters.*
>
> *He restores my soul;*
>
> *He leads me in the paths of righteousness*
>
> *For His name's sake.*

The NIV uses the word "refreshes".

But I think the word "restores" is more powerful.

Before I came to believe in Jesus, I was worn out. Totally. My neck, back and knees were not in good shape. I went up and downstairs by crawling or on my bottom. I couldn't raise my arm very high, which led to problems writing on the blackboard.

In came Jesus. A friend told me about quiet times with God. I embraced the idea of a quiet time. Even though I felt restless when I sat, I did it anyway. Soon I could feel the peace of God come over me. Gradually those aches and pains started to disappear. With this feeling of peace came healing.

I have heard arguments saying, "But I can't find time – uninterrupted time to spend with God." I couldn't either. If I tried to have a moment of peace when the family was awake it would not work.

I asked God to wake me up earlier if He wanted this time with me.

Well, He did. I said, "Please wake me up God if you want me up."

After that prayer at night, I awoke refreshed and the clock said: 6:00 am. That was an hour earlier than I needed to wake up. You have to visualize my surprise. But I didn't hesitate. I got right up because God called me. I knew I needed to go to Him. And I did.

My first few times of trying to sit still, actually more than a few, I didn't last long in a quiet position. It's still hard for me to sit still. But I read the Bible. I wrote my thoughts. I prayed in my journal. And I started to grow closer to God.

And I started to relax.

I learned that He would control everything – if I would let Him.

Psalm 103:1-5 says it all:

> *A Psalm of David. Bless the Lord, O my soul; And all that is within me, bless His holy name!*
>
> *Bless the Lord, O my soul, And forget not all His benefits:*
>
> *Who forgives all your iniquities, Who heals all your diseases,*
>
> *Who redeems your life from destruction, Who crowns you with lovingkindness and tender mercies,*
>
> *Who satisfies your mouth with good things, So that your youth is renewed like the eagle's. (NKJV)*

If you want to be healed of stress, anger, or anything that has you tied in knots, may I suggest you go to Jesus? Go and rest in Him. Let Him bring about the peace you crave.

Let God restore you.

He can restore you into His Presence. He can restore you physically. He can restore you mentally.
Just come to Him.

Matthew 11:28-30 from The Message:

> *Are you tired? Worn out? Burned out on religion? Come to me. Get away with me and you'll recover your life. I'll show you how to take a real rest.*
>
> *Walk with me and work with me—watch how I do it. Learn the unforced rhythms of grace. I won't lay anything heavy or ill-fitting on you.*
>
> *Keep company with me and you'll learn to live freely and lightly." (MSG)*

May I pray for you and me?

Lord Jesus, You are the Healer, the Restorer, the Comforter. I want to be in Your presence. Help me to get there. Teach me how to listen to You.

Teach me to be still before You. Teach me to come to You. In Jesus' name. Amen

Find a quiet spot and pray.
Then listen to what God has to say.
If you don't wake early enough, ask God to wake you up.
Be refreshed and ready to come to Him and be restored.
Read His Word and grow.

Journal Your Thoughts

Does God Really Want to Meet with Me?

As I thought back to 20 years ago, before I knew Who Jesus is, I tried to remember what it was like. My journey of discovery is another tale but as I started to say my "yes" to Jesus, things started to change.

It started with small things.

I didn't get as upset when circumstances didn't go the way I planned. It did take reminders. I made sure I kept those daily reminders from God's Word so that I could spend time with Him throughout the day when things didn't go the way I wanted them.

I started to see myself as God saw me. I didn't like what God and I saw. I asked for help to make me be more Christ-like.

It's been a struggle and sometimes it seems so slow.

But I think I am finally letting myself go – I am giving up on being right, being ahead, and instead I work to serve others. It is not at all easy for a striver, a doer, and a proactive person.

To be in a state of non-activity is very hard for me. I don't like it at all.

But I know I need it. As a result, I sit. To ponder, to think, to pray. I wait. I listen.

Are those words coming into my head from me?

I don't think the words are coming from me. They sound different. They sound more powerful than I feel. They sound like God.

I ask God about things all the time. I didn't use to. I used to do my own thing and when I got into trouble then I would ask God. Is that post prayer? Oh Lord, what are You going to do about this – that I got myself in trouble for?

Have you ever taken on tasks without hearing from God first? I have. And the results are usually dismal.

In my children's book, *The Kingdom of Thrim*, the protagonist who is happy and content with life, his creativity and friends, decides very quickly, on a whim, to head off with the antagonist to find a better life. He didn't ask God. There's the main point. But then even in this dire predicament, he finds himself in – it isn't too late. God hears and answers.

It is never too late to ask God for help.

He is always there. Always ready to listen.

I heard these words in my mind – I think God is speaking.

Cast down your crowns,
So, I can approach you

*I can only get close
when your heart is soft,
your mind is open.*

*When nothing stands
Between us.*

*When you humbly fall down
On your knees
I will approach you
I AM
Wants to meet you.*

There are 5 verbs in **Psalm 113** that resonate with me.

> *Who is like the LORD our God, the One who sits enthroned on high, who stoops down to look on the heavens and the earth?*
>
> *He raises the poor from the dust and lifts the needy from the ash heap;*
>
> *he seats them with princes, with the princes of his people.*
>
> *He settles the childless woman in her home as a happy mother of children. Praise the LORD.
> (Psalm 113:5-9)*

God stoops

Wow, that's powerful. God lowers Himself to be with His people. And the biggest stoop came when He came as Jesus – to the earth.

God raises

He takes people who are nothing and makes them powerful. Think of King David a lowly shepherd, Daniel – a refugee in a foreign country, Joseph – who rose to mighty power in Egypt.

God lifts

No matter how low we become, God can lift us. No matter how dirty or sinful we feel, He accepts us and lifts us from the miry clay.

God seats

It doesn't matter to God whether we are rich or poor, powerful or humble, young or old, needy or wealthy – we can sit with Him at His banqueting table.

God settles

God wants things to be right. When things don't go right, He works at setting things straight.

Do you want to meet your God in a closer setting?
Do you want to dig deeper into His Word?

May I pray for you and me?

Lord Jesus, deep in each of our hearts, we long for a closer connection to You. Help us to find that way by reading Your Word regularly. Help us to join with others to discuss what we find. Help us to listen quietly so we can hear You speak. In Jesus' name. Amen.

How close is your relationship with God?
Have you accepted Jesus as your Lord and Saviour?
Study the Bible and pray – see what God tells you.

Journal Your Thoughts

How Not to Be Held Captive by Fear

Fear

The wind howled. The rain pelted. The thunder cracked. The sky grew darker. Then bang…

I used to fear a lot. Fear kept me from doing many things. I didn't like to eat at a restaurant alone or even with my kids. I didn't want to travel anywhere by myself. I felt trapped inside a box of distress. It kept me from moving forward where God wanted me.

It wasn't until I released all of this to Jesus that all my fears started to fade away.

I think the worst fear happened after a thunderstorm.

Lightning struck our boathouse. The pressure blew the door from its hinges and pieces of wood flew across the front lawn. Lightening hit the tree beside our boathouse. Everything inside the boathouse broke apart. The cord to the refrigerator completely disintegrated.

The front doors of the boathouse flew open. Praise the Lord, we had taken the boat to the marina for repairs the week prior or it would have been ruined.

Back inside the house, we were huddled under doorframes. The wind blew ferociously as well, and we thought it safer to be under something strong and solid. The cottage rattled. We heard a humungous crash and bang (I guess that was the door flying off). Right at that moment, my middle daughter stated, "I have to go to the bathroom." There was no stopping her. Later I realized that could have been fatal if the energy from the strike hit the toilet.

Then BANG. I heard the loudest boom possible. And crack. And then… silence. As quickly as all that happened everything fell silent. No more wind. No more rain. No more noise. We went outside to assess the damage. That week my hubby decided to stay in the city. There we were 4 – myself, my two daughters, and my daughter's friend. And our little Bichon dog, Simon.

As we returned to the cottage, I continued to prepare the dinner that sat on the stove. There was no power, but we thought we would eat cold spaghetti.

As we started eating my daughter's friend yelled, "Stop! There is glass in the food."

The light bulb on the wall that shows any septic problems had blown completely apart.

Quickly throwing out the night's meal I sent the oldest ones back to the lodge where they were working. My youngest, our dog and I set off for another lodge down the road to stay overnight until we could get repairs started.

Both the line to the phone and the line to the electricity had melted on the pole. Branches were everywhere.

But we were all okay.

Maybe. Everyone seemed to survive it well except me. For the next few years every time I heard thunder I shook and escaped to where I couldn't hear it. I wouldn't go outside if there was even a threat of rain or thunder.

We did learn important safety considerations to keep during thunderstorms. Take cover. Close all windows. We learned that lightning likes the path of least resistance. Don't use the washroom during a severe thunderstorm. Keep away from the windows.

It took me over five years, some hypnotherapy and of course finding Jesus to help get this fear behind me. I am quite calm during a thunderstorm now especially if I am inside.

Here is my prayer for those of you who have fears:

Lord Jesus, we know You are in control of all things. We ask for safety during times of trouble. But we know that even in dire situations You will be there. You have this all covered. We will be with You forever. Trusting in You can build a peace inside us that cannot be shattered.

Many of your passages in Your Word address fear. You know fear is a great weakness of ours. Help us to give these fears over to You. You tell us to be anxious for nothing. And that means no thing. There is nothing that can come between us. We call upon Your peace to descend on us. You say to not let our hearts be troubled. So come Lord Jesus and comfort our troubled hearts – make them new and free.

Let us come before you now in our hearts and minds and release to You anything and everything that is holding us back from our potential. We want to glorify You. We need to be fully alive to do what we are called to do. Release these fears. In Jesus' name. Amen.

If you have fears, ask Jesus to show you how to release them to Him. Read scripture passages that are about fear. The word fear is mentioned more than 400 times. God knows we need to have His assurances.

Here are 8 scriptures to help you recall that there is no fear when we trust in the Lord. Write them out on cards. Draw them in your Bible. Paint them. Memorize them. Live them.

Psalm 23:4

> *Even though I walk through the valley of the shadow of death, I will fear no evil, for you are with me; your rod and your staff, they comfort me. (ESV)*

Isaiah 41:13

For I am the Lord your God

  who takes hold of your right hand

and says to you, Do not fear;

  I will help you.

Exodus 14:13

Moses answered the people, "Do not be afraid. Stand firm and you will see the deliverance the Lord will bring you today. The Egyptians you see today you will never see again."

Deuteronomy 31:6

Be strong and courageous. Do not be afraid or terrified because of them, for the Lord your God goes with you; he will never leave you nor forsake you.

2 Timothy 1:7

For God has not given us a spirit of fear, but of power and of love and of a sound mind. (NKJV)

Psalm 27:1

> *The Lord is my light and my salvation—whom shall I fear? The Lord is the stronghold of my life—of whom shall I be afraid?*

Romans 8:15

> *The Spirit you received does not make you slaves, so that you live in fear again; rather, the Spirit you received brought about your adoption to sonship. And by him we cry, "Abba, Father."*

Philippians 4:6-7

> *Do not be anxious about anything, but in every situation, by prayer and petition, with thanksgiving, present your requests to God. And the peace of God, which transcends all understanding, will guard your hearts and your minds in Christ Jesus.*

Journal Your Thoughts

Can You Follow the Holy Spirit?

We used to visit North Carolina with our family and stay along the ocean. What I remember vividly were the winds. Sometimes on shore; sometimes offshore.

I thought today of how wind can affect how far our speech carries. Try shouting when the wind is at your back; then shout when you are facing into it. As the wind blew out to sea, our voices caught the wind and travelled far out. However, when the wind blew at us, we couldn't even hear ourselves speak. Our words were flung away.

I view the Holy Spirit as a spiritual wind.

If we are following Christ, we will be in a favourable position for our words to carry His message to those He wants to hear.

Sometimes when I feel frustrated with what I am doing or saying it's a wake-up call to check which way I am facing. Is the Holy Spirit behind me?

Like the earthly winds, the Holy Spirit doesn't have a pattern. We can't predict where it will blow us.

John 3:7-8

So, don't be so surprised when I tell you that you have to be 'born from above'—out of this world, so to speak.

> *You know well enough how the wind blows this way and that. You hear it rustling through the trees, but you have no idea where it comes from or where it's headed next.*
>
> *That's the way it is with everyone 'born from above' by the wind of God, the Spirit of God.*
> *(MSG)*

Taking time to sit and read God's Word, asking for answers and listening for answers are essential elements to help us let the Holy Spirit move us along.

Are you being blown by the wind of God?

My friend, an author-singer songwriter, Sally Meadows, has written a worship song called Holy Spirit that always touches my heart when I hear it.
Listen to a few of the words and see if you are blowing along with the Holy Spirit.

Holy Spirit

It doesn't matter who we are
You welcome everyone into Your arms
And as You shine Your guiding light
We'll be on our knees and then we will rise!

Holy Spirit, Holy Spirit
Come and open up and fill our hearts with love [iv]

May I pray for you and me?

Father help us to let the Holy Spirit guide us in our actions, deeds and thoughts. Help us to know if we are facing the wrong way. Turn us around so we can follow Your will and glorify you. In Jesus' name. Amen.

Stop and listen and if you are facing the wrong way, let the Holy Spirit guide you along the right path. Remember to stay rooted by reading God's Word.

Journal Your Thoughts

Who Me? Deny Myself?

I use a devotional called *My Utmost for His Highest* by Oswald Chambers. I've read it so much one copy is falling apart.

I heard a great sermon the other day – it made me think. And to top it off I read Oswald Chambers the same day – same topic.

Is God telling me something?

Then I read it on Facebook. Yikes.

The topic is self. Yes, me.

Jesus said in **Matthew 16:24:**

> *Then Jesus said to his disciples, "Whoever wants to be my disciple must deny themselves and take up their cross and follow me." (NIV)*

Yes, Jesus said to deny myself. But thank goodness our minister explained it as it makes it sound like just forget about me.

Our minister said God made me, made my complete person, my identity. My job is to discover that identity in Christ. But at the same time, I have to remember that I must deny feelings, emotions and thoughts that are driven by the world or by Satan. I have to keep myself pure for God. I can't just do as I feel I want to, just because I can do it. I need to ask God and follow His leading.

This is tough.

We were told to beware of people who like to manipulate scripture to make you do something they want you to do.

I do remember a time when I was picking someone up to drive a long distance (six hours) through traffic and we wouldn't arrive until late in the evening. It took me two hours to drive to her house. Someone arrived unexpectedly and needed a ride. My friend told me I should drive that person to a place further southeast and we were travelling southwest.

The friend was able to take public transportation.

I said I didn't feel like I should do this as I wanted to arrive in time and driving through the city would make us even later. And of course, I am not a great city driver. The whole thing made me anxious. Well, she finally did put her friend on the public transit. But she kept nattering at me with the fact that I should be doing as God wished. I should have denied myself and taken this friend instead.

I have thought and prayed about this situation over the years. I still believe that I didn't feel called to drive her friend. The circumstances made perfect sense to me – I said I would pick her up and take her to the meeting. But she used the scripture of "denying myself" to justify actions that she wanted me to take.

I believe that forgetting about myself means to be aware where God wants me to go and what He wants me to do. It doesn't mean someone else telling me what to do. I have communication with God. I feel at peace when I make a decision. If not, I know something is not right.

But I have to be aware of me – before I can make tough decisions.

If people can manipulate me, then it is not right.

Certainly, Jesus meant that I shouldn't always be thinking of myself.

Oswald Chambers says:

> *Our Lord's teaching is anti-self-realization.*

All the new age books on the shelf are pushing people towards finding themselves. We need to find God – then we will know ourselves through His revelation. Being aware of who we are; what we need to change; and liking who God made us are important.

May I pray for you and me?

Father, Creator, the One Who made us, help us to be the people You want us to be. Help us learn to listen to You so we can find our way and our peace. Help us learn to forget about ourselves in order to follow You when You call. In Jesus' name. Amen.

Think about this scripture.
Is it calling you towards God?
Does it speak to you about who you are in Christ?
Read more of the Bible each day.

Journal Your Thoughts

How to Live Vicariously Through Christ

I want to live vicariously through Christ.

That thought came to me the other day while meditating. I looked up the word vicariously to see what it meant.

Vicariously means committed or entrusted.

That's exactly what I want to do.
It also means to experience one through another. That means God in us and we in Him. Because we are united to Him by His Spirit.

There seem to be some facets of my life that are at odds with one another – my will and my sinful nature.

I used to think my will was wrong. But I don't feel that way any longer.

Oswald Chambers says:

> *The will is the essential element in God's creation of man; sin is a perverse disposition which entered into man.* [vi]

I like that. My will is an essential element of my life and God made it especially for me.

It's a case of who runs my will.

Therefore, my dear friends, as you have always obeyed—not only in my presence, but now much more in my absence—continue to work out your salvation with fear and trembling, for it is God who works in you to will and to act in order to fulfill his good purpose. (Philippians 2:12-13)

We hear that God works in us through our will to act for His purposes.

Here is The Message translation.

What I'm getting at, friends, is that you should simply keep on doing what you've done from the beginning.

When I was living among you, you lived in responsive obedience.

Now that I'm separated from you, keep it up. Better yet, redouble your efforts.

Be energetic in your life of salvation, reverent and sensitive before God.

That energy is God's energy, an energy deep within you, God himself willing and working at what will

> *give him the most pleasure. (Philippians 2:12-13, MSG)*

I can feel that. I can understand that.

Each day I learn something new. A new shoot or growth in my life.

Today I read from **Galatians 4:6.**

> *Because you are his sons, God sent the Spirit of his Son into our hearts, the Spirit who calls out, "Abba, Father."*

I'm not sure why that verse made an impact today. But now it is crystal clear to me.

The Holy Spirit is the Spirit of Jesus.

I like that. That's how Jesus lives in me vicariously.

I committed my life to Christ, so He came in the form of the Holy Spirit to dwell in me.

I'm sure I've heard this before but today, through reading God's Word – I worked it out. That's why Jesus lives in me.

Now when I read this statement from Oswald Chambers it all makes sense.

God is the source of your will, therefore you are able to work out His will. ^{vii}

Yes.

Now I realize that salvation is a process and each day as I study and pray, God opens another nugget for me to chew on.

Are you working out your salvation with God?
Let Him live vicariously through you.

May I pray for you and me?

Lord Jesus, first of all, thank You for leaving us Your Holy Spirit to teach and guide us. Thank You, too, for Your Word that opens so many doors that help our wills get closer to Your will. Help us to seek You and follow You vicariously this week. In Your Name, Jesus. Amen.

What nuggets is God teaching you today?
Are you going to match your will to His?

Journal Your Thoughts

Ask a Fortune Teller?

Is there a way out of this darkness we find ourselves in?

In my study of Isaiah, I see many familiarities with our situations today.

Isaiah 8:19

> *When people tell you, "Try out the fortunetellers.*
>
> *Consult the spiritualists.*
>
> *Why not tap into the spirit-world,*
>
> *get in touch with the dead?" (MSG)*

Does this sound familiar?

Have you read the papers? Have you read the Internet? There are always pages for Astrology. People ask, "What sign are you?" And there are still fortune tellers too.

The word "luck" is bandied about everywhere. "Good luck." "Oh, you were lucky". "As luck would have it."

During this time in Bible history, the people lost their belief in God. They searched for answers in other places. But they were the wrong places. They suffered from invasion and hunger. They felt distressed with all that was happening around them.

Today we see the distress in people – God's people too. Are they looking in the right places? I think maybe not.

Look at the books lining the shelves in the "self-help" section of the bookstores. Look at all the new age therapies.

Interestingly, the secular world is talking about meditation, peace, focus, commitment, community, love, friendships. Don't those sound similar to the terms from God's Word?

But did the Israelites ask God for help?
Did they humble themselves to acknowledge the need for God?

Where does the world look for answers?

They look to movie stars, sports stars, scientists, businessmen and the charismatic words of leaders.

Did the people of Israel do the same thing? YES

Isaiah 8:21-22

> *Frustrated and famished,*
>
> > *they try one thing after another.*
>
> *When nothing works out they get angry,*
>
> > *cursing first this god and then that one,*

Looking this way and that,

> *up, down, and sideways—and seeing nothing,*

A blank wall, an empty hole.

> *They end up in the dark with nothing. (MSG)*

But where does Isaiah tell them to look?

Isaiah 8:20

> *Tell them, "No, we're going to study the Scriptures. People who try the other ways get nowhere - a dead end! (MSG)*

They are to look to the Scriptures – God's Word. We are blessed with the Old Testament and the New Testament.

How are we going to get out of the darkness in this world?

The same way as Isaiah told God's people.

Ask God and study His Word.

This is relevant for us today. If you are in distress, cry out to God and study His Word in the Bible.

The people in Isaiah's time did not have the light of Jesus yet. We do. We have no excuses.

We have Father, Son and Holy Spirit – our Triune God. We can speak and ask directly to God through Jesus. We can freely study the Word of God. We have no reasons to live in darkness. The Light has come. The Light is here. Thanks be to God.

May I pray for you and me?

Lord Jesus, we acknowledge that we need you. We desperately need you. Please enter into our thoughts, our emotions and our actions. Teach us to ask for help and teach us that daily reading of Your Word will strengthen and guide us. In Your Name, Jesus I pray. Amen.

If you feel you are in darkness, look to the light of Jesus.
Ask Him to reveal Himself to you.
Pick up a Bible and start reading.

Journal Your Thoughts

Why Are You Poisoning Yourself?

I was hurt, very hurt.

Someone said an untruth that bothered me tremendously. I felt angry, betrayed and resentful. Everything I said and touched started to turn to stone. My heart became hardened. I wanted to feel the anger – conversations always led back to how hurt I felt. I knew it was wrong. I felt torn in two, worn out. What could I do?

I recall those feelings now. I don't have them anymore. I was able to forgive and find peace. How? How did I do that? Here are six things you need to know before you can start on the road to forgiveness.

Let go.

Yes, let go. Forgiveness means a decision to let go of resentment or anger. It does not mean a denial of what happened or that the act is justified.

But we need to LET GO.

How can we do that? Did you hear that the definition says that we don't need to condone what was done? But we need to let go of it. It is something that will happen supernaturally as you follow through these steps. But you need to keep it in the front of your mind as I go through the steps. Remember let go.

Ask yourself, "What are the pitfalls of unforgiveness?"

You may ask what if I do forgive, how will that help me? I want to stay angry. I feel like I deserve the right to be angry. I've been hurt and want to feel the pain.

My answer is, you do have that right to keep the anger. We have free will. But what does anger do to you, to your body, mind and soul? It does everything you don't want it to do. It makes you sick. You may ache physically from tenseness. You may have headaches, fatigue, weight gain, weight loss, or depression. These are things that could happen if you keep the anger.

Proverbs 14:30

> *A sound mind makes for a robust body,*
>
> *but runaway emotions corrode the bones. (MSG)*

That doesn't sound too delightful, does it? Corroding of the bones, brittle bones, disintegrating, useless.

What will you miss if you don't forgive?

Check out what you may be missing without forgiving.

There are good things that happen to you when you forgive. Besides better health, your face changes, you smile more often. You see goodness around you (by the way, it was there before).

And as a Christian how do we want others to see us – as angry, or as loving, peacemaking people? God wants us to forgive others and He says that unless we do so how will God forgive us of our sins (and we do have them, don't we?).

Matthew 5:8

> *You're blessed when you get your inside world - your mind and heart - put right. Then you can see God in the outside world. (MSG)*

We lose touch with God when our minds and hearts are out of whack. When we are fraught with anxiety, fear and anger we can't find God. Unforgiveness does that; it blocks the goodness around us. It blocks our relationship with God.

Get over yourself and think of others

Be kind to your friends and become a loving person once again. If you are truthful, you will hear how you are acting around others. Remember we are all filled with sin. If someone has sinned against you, be a peacemaker and forgive them so that when the tables are turned, you too will receive forgiveness.

Don't fret the small stuff

We are not perfect – not one of us. How do you know when you are going to go down that path and do something to someone else? You may not even know it and they might be upset with something you said and did. So really, don't fret the small stuff. Many other things will happen and this area that is upsetting you now will seem trivial in the future. Remember the saying, "Do unto others as you would have them do to you." (Luke 6:31)

Ask God

This really should be step one, but you needed to learn to give up the unforgiveness before I gave you this step. Ask God for help. He can't change your emotions, but He can help you change them, He can help you find peace, He can help you know Him and His ways which are higher than any other way.

If God says to do it, do it. And do it right now. Don't wait because God says we are to do it right away and not to let the sun go down. Get rid of it – now. Ask God to help you get rid of this unforgiveness and then release it to Him, right now.

Ephesians 4:26-27

> *Go ahead and be angry. You do well to be angry—but don't use your anger as fuel for revenge. And don't stay angry. Don't go to bed*

angry. Don't give the Devil that kind of foothold in your life. (MSG)

I will be praying for everyone who is harbouring a grudge or living in an unforgiving state. Give yourself a break and give it over to God.

May I pray for you and me?

Lord, this unforgiveness is one of the hardest things we face in our life here on earth. You talked about it in Your Word. You said we have to forgive. Period. So, Lord, I give over any feelings, emotions, or hardness of heart that I have residing in me. I ask You to cleanse me of all of it. Even the stuff I don't know about. Give me a clean heart before you. In Jesus' name. Amen.

Read Colossians 3:13.

Bear with each other and forgive one another if any of you has a grievance against someone. Forgive as the Lord forgave you.

Other Resources to Help You

Meyer, Joyce. "Six Ways to Find Unforgiveness and Remove It: Everyday Answers." Joyce Meyer Ministries. Accessed February 8, 2020.

https://joycemeyer.org/everydayanswers/ea-teachings/six-ways-to-find-unforgiveness-and-remove-it.

The word forgive: Forgiveness can be defined as the decision to let go of resentment, anger, and thoughts of revenge as a result of a real, or perceived offence, hurt, or wrongdoing against you. Forgiving someone does not mean denying a person's responsibility for hurting you, nor does it mean minimizing, or justifying the act.

"Forgiveness and Letting Go How to Achieve It." Essential Life Skills.net. Accessed February 8, 2020.

https://www.essentiallifeskills.net/forgiveness-and-letting-go.html.

Journal Your Thoughts

How and Why I Should Stop Saying the "S" Word

I never thought about it. It never occurred to me. My daughter said, "Mom you really shouldn't say that "s" word." Now before you start thinking that the "s" word was a swear word – it isn't.

The word she meant was "stupid". She has taught her children not to say that "s" word or the "d" word either – yes – dumb.

Frederick William Faber, a noted English hymn writer and theologian, whose best-known work is Faith of Our Fathers is quoted to have said:

> *With the help of grace, the habit of saying kind words is very quickly formed, and when once formed, it is not speedily lost.* [viii]

I like the fact that he says saying kind words is a habit we need to form and that once formed we hold on to that.

Therefore, it is so important that we not only teach our children to speak kind words but we as spouses, friends, and grandparents use words that we would like our children to get into the habit of using. And certainly not use words that we would not want to hear our children repeating.

We are told in God's Word, in **Proverbs 16:24:**

Kind words are like honey sweet to the soul and healthy for the body. (NLT)

When I first became a Christian, even though I didn't swear very often, I started to notice that I still was capable of a rant with words that were not "honey to the soul". This was a choice I made. Could I think before opening my mouth and not speak unkind words even when I felt angry and frustrated?

Choices: We make them every day, sometimes every minute.

Proverbs 15:23 says:

Everyone enjoys a fitting reply; it is wonderful to say the right thing at the right time! (NLT)

I don't know about you but sometimes I answer without thinking it through. Certainly, email and texting have added to this haste to speak without deep thought. How can we make a "fitting reply" when we are hurried to text back, or answer an email?

God can help us change if we
ask Him. But we have to be willing to do the work.

Proverbs 10:20

The speech of a good person is worth waiting for;

the blabber of the wicked is worthless. (MSG)

How can we, in our hurried lives, learn to speak slowly, carefully and wisely?

Here are three ways I think will help us in this growth:

Slow down

I think that is what God is telling us. It is worth waiting for the wise speech of a good person. They have thought through their words, carefully crafting the best way to explain something. They have prayed that God will bless those words.

Stop answering emails and texts right away. Give it a few minutes at least, so you can think over your replies especially if someone is seeking advice or has said something that you disagree with.

Wake up with God

When you wake up, ask God to watch over your mouth for the entire day. Ask Him to speak to you, if He senses you are going to make bad choices. And then be ready to listen to Him.

Bite your tongue or count to ten

Don't react right away when confronted with anger, or disagreement. If necessary, ask to be excused to the washroom (if this is a face-to-face meeting) and in that time – pray that God will calm your spirit, give you wisdom and give you peace.

Throughout Proverbs, we are given Scripture after Scripture about the power of words. They can build up and tear down. They can cause division and hatred. They can bring reconciliation and love.

What do your words do?

May I pray for you and me?

Lord, You gave us the power of speech and the ability to think what we say. No other living creature that You created can do this. Let us use this gift wisely to show love, care and protection of one another. In Jesus' name. Amen

Think about your words this week.
Pray every morning for revelation.
Learn to curb your impulses and speak with wisdom and love.
And stay reading His Word.

Journal Your Thoughts

What Happens When the Fire Alarm is Pulled?

Teaching rules to children and adults.

The players on the hockey rink raced for the puck. Almost a goal. They regrouped and one player headed down the ice. All of a sudden, a bell rang. A loud bell. It wasn't a goal. It was the fire alarm. We as spectators looked at each other. What do we do? We waited to see if it would be shut off. No, still a loud ringing.

We headed outdoors. They evacuated the whole arena. Firetruck sirens could be heard in the distance. No smoke. What was going on?

The truth was that a young boy pulled the alarm. Why? Because it was there, I guess. Of course, the parents were distraught to think that their child caused such a commotion. They were very upset with the child.

But afterwards, they began to think – "Did we ever tell him not to pull that bright shiny red handle?"

The child knew he did something wrong. He asked for forgiveness. It was accepted but the parents also learned that more teaching was necessary.

When teaching children, we need to be specific and repetitive.

I remember this saying to teach me how to cross the road safely.

Walk don't run when you cross the street
Use your eyes, use your ears.
Then you use your feet.

And how many of you were taught fire rules, fire safety. Do you remember the phrase, "stop and drop, feel the door to see if it's hot, find the nearest but safest exit"?

And what about how to be safe from strangers?

We need to be specific and give examples.

What would you do it a person came up to you and said, "Your mommy is really hurt? You must come with me right away."

That can be emotionally gripping, and your child may not understand that it was not safe to follow that person. They need to be told what to do in each situation that might occur. Our family used a code word that only our family knew. And the person would need to say that word for our children to feel safe to go with that person. Nowadays kids carry cell phones and checking in with mom or dad would be the first line of defence.

These are all examples of rules that we learned as children and need to teach our children.

God has the same plan – to teach His children.
And He has the rule book too – our Bible.

Besides learning His Word, we are told to teach it to our children.

Proverbs 22:6

> *Train up a child in the way he should go.*
> *(NASV)*

Deuteronomy 6:6-7

> *These commandments that I give you today are to be on your hearts. Impress them on your children. Talk about them when you sit at home and when you walk along the road, when you lie down and when you get up.*

Remember I said to be specific. When you are studying God's Word, I have found that if I listen to God, He shows me what to read and study.

At the moment I am looking at creativity passages. God created us for a purpose and with special gifts to glorify Him.

What are you studying?

His promises?
Prayer passages?
Strength?
Forgiveness?

There are so many – find what you need and study it.

We need repetition.

And also, I said, that as parents we need to be repetitive in our teaching.

Learning scripture passages helps us when we need to recall God's Word:

For instance, now I can say:

Do not be anxious – Philippians 4:6
The Spirit of God made me – Job 33:4
For we are God's workmanship – Ephesians 2:10
Trust in the Lord with all your heart – Proverbs 3:5

As children or adults, we are all children of God who need to learn how to live safely, peacefully and by being specific and intentional in our studies, and repetitive by memorizing we will be better equipped to work for God's glory here on earth.

May I pray for you and me?

Lord Jesus, we know, as Your children, we want to follow Your Way. We don't always know the rules. We don't always follow them when we know them. Forgive us. But You have given us the guide in the Bible. Your words are living and active when we read and study. Help us to give priority to seeking to know more by studying scripture. In Jesus' name. Amen.

Decide on the passage or passages that God is calling for you to study.
Read and memorize and seek God's help in all you do.

Journal Your Thoughts

Travel to the End of the Known Universe and What is Found?

I love the fall. After a rainy summer, the sun has shone for many days. Light winds and warm temperatures continue with blue skies.

We began our fall clean up the other day. Leaves needed to be picked up. All the outside decorations and chairs are stored away. It looks rather empty.

As I look at the landscape with the leaves changing colours and then falling back to earth, I am reminded that life is a series of rhythms.

We have busy days like celebrating Thanksgiving with our family. We have slower days recouping from all the fun.

**But through everything,
we can see and know that God is visible.**

I watched a movie by Louie Giglio on the immensity of God's Creation and how small we are. What a mighty God!

Everything is made perfectly. The sun is the exact distance from the earth to sustain life. We have daylight and at night we have the stars and the moon.

God cares so much for us. He breathed life into us at birth and then again at our rebirth when we accept Jesus as Lord and Saviour.

Genesis 2:7

> *Then the LORD God formed a man from the dust of the ground and breathed into his nostrils the breath of life, and the man became a living being.*

John 20:22

> *And with that he (Jesus) breathed on them and said, "Receive the Holy Spirit."*

I love the passage in the Bible where it states that Christ holds everything together.

Colossians 1:17

> *He (Jesus) is before all things, and in him all things hold together.*

When you watch the movie from Louie Giglio you will see something very surprising. At the end of the universe, as we know it, through the Hubble telescope, there is a cross. Yes, a cross.

That's outstanding, isn't it?

I believe we can be at peace through all the turmoil, the death and destruction because God knows it all, and He loves us.

God is in control at all times.

We can remember that if we get to know Him.

If you haven't asked Jesus to be a part of your life, do it now. It's simple. Say this:

Jesus, I need you.
Jesus, I'm sorry. I know I can't do this life by myself.
Jesus, come and be my Saviour.

Then tell someone. Learn to study God's Word and talk to Him in prayer.

God is. God was. God will be. Through all eternity we have a Saviour.

May I pray for you and me?

Lord, in our small minds and hearts it's hard for us to comprehend the majesty and power of Who You are. We ask forgiveness for our shortcomings and accept the grace You so lavish upon us. As we breathe in Your love and power, help us to shine for others so they too can know You. In Jesus' name. Amen.

Remember to talk to God.

Honestly talk to Him.
He is big enough to listen to even the tiniest of your problems and powerful enough to fix them.
Read His Word and expand your knowledge of Who God is.

Journal Your Thoughts

What Made My Husband Mutter, "Yes, dear", All the Time?

I didn't realize I acted like a control freak.

After troubles with a babysitter when our children were young, I assumed control. I wanted to know exactly where each child was going, whom they were with and what time they'd be home.

These were good questions, but I acted like a drill sergeant and made normal discussions into battles. My fear for my kids made me want to micromanage every single aspect of their lives.

Thankfully I found a great new church, a mentor, a Bible study and eventually I found Jesus.

It was during this time that I realized there was a hidden fault. Hidden to me – not to God and maybe not to others. I could now see how much I frustrated my husband and my kids with this control issue.

My hubby started to say, "Yes, dear" to everything. The kids argued with anything and everything I said.

Enter Jesus. I started to read His Word. He showed me that God was in control – not me.

Psalm 19:12

> *But who can discern their own errors? Forgive my hidden faults.*

I didn't know that I didn't realize I sinned.

When the truth became evident to me, I asked God for forgiveness for my lack of trust in Him. Then things started to change slowly– but for the better.

I started to be aware of this control tendency. But I wanted to find out why I did it and how I could change.

It wasn't easy.

I'm happy to report that very rarely now does my hubby say, "Yes, dear." Since we are both firstborn, we learned to listen better to each other and both of us bend a little.

My youngest daughter's friend said to her, "What happened to your mom? She is nicer."

I knew that my wanting to control would be an issue for the rest of my life. But it is something that God wants me to work on.

But then I read:

1 Corinthians 4:4

My conscience is clear, but that does not make me innocent. It is the Lord who judges me.

God forgave me my lack of knowledge about this problem.

But what other hidden faults did I have buried deep?

There are still hidden faults that I haven't seen yet. God knows them and will show them to me.

I must keep studying and listening to God to get to the deepest parts of me.

Thank the Lord, the blood of Jesus covers me and by His grace, I am forgiven even for my hidden sins.

I believe God still wants me to uncover my hidden sins. The sin of control is only one of many that God has revealed to me over the years.

And just like addictions I am never completely cured. I have to keep on being aware and asking for God's help.

May I pray for you and me?

Father, thank You for allowing Jesus to die for our sins. Thank You for Your grace and mercy. Help us to uncover anything that does not glorify You. In Jesus' name. Amen.

Ask God to reveal the true nature of your heart.
Is there something lurking there that you need to see and work on?
Read the Bible and learn more about God and yourself.

Journal Your Thoughts

How a Hearing Loss Taught Me to Listen to God

"You can't hear!"

For several years, my kids kept telling me that I needed hearing aids. I kept telling them that they were mumbling. I could hear fine. I thought.

But after much grumbling from my family, I finally made an appointment. The audiologist thought I could benefit from hearing aids, but I needed to visit an Ear Nose and Throat Specialist first – I'll call him my ENT.

My first visit to the ENT resulted in nothing. Nothing wrong with my ears. Come back in two years he said and that was after he stuck a scope down my throat. I don't have a clue why the doctor needed to do that to check my ears.

Another two years went by, and the grumbling from the family increased. I also began to realize I couldn't hear in small groups. I decided to revisit my audiologist. He found the same hearing loss and now was concerned with a significant drop of hearing in my left ear. And he wanted to rule out a tumour.

He also looked at my mother's records and found my hearing profile matched hers. He believed it was hereditary and he suggested I book an appointment with a different ENT this time as I was not happy with the first one.

Another problem arose though. Now we were leaving to spend six months in the south for winter. I needed to wait until I came back in the spring to have the appointment. Then after the appointment, I waited again until I could find the result. Finally. Good news. There was nothing wrong. I just couldn't hear.

Now I could finally get hearing aids. And that has worked very well. After a little bit of trouble at the beginning, I am now used to wearing them. I can hear everything said in small groups. I watch movies again without saying, "What did he say?"

This entire lesson has taught me that we have to pay attention to our hearing.

It's very important and I urge you if you think you may have a problem, get it checked.
But all this discussion of hearing made me aware of how much we must listen to God. Most of us, including me, talk a long streak to God. But how many of us focus on listening to Him. And how?

How can we hear from Him?

Lately, I have tried a new strategy. I write my prayers down, all that is on my mind and my thoughts from studying the Bible. Then I STOP and I concentrate on listening to what God is telling me. I ready my pen now because I know I will need to record what He says. It fascinates me with what He tells me when I read over what I have written. It's like taking dictation.

The Bible is full of Scriptures that tell us to listen to God.

> *So faith comes from hearing, and hearing through the word of Christ. (Romans 10:17, ESV)*

I love **Proverbs 2:1-5**

> *My son, if you accept my words*
>   *and store up my commands within you,*
> *turning your ear to wisdom*
>   *and applying your heart to understanding—*
> *indeed, if you call out for insight*
>   *and cry aloud for understanding,*
> *and if you look for it as for silver*
>   *and search for it as for hidden treasure,*

> *then you will understand the fear of the Lord*
>
> *and find the knowledge of God.*

I find that I am having wonderful conversations with God. Two-way conversations.

Now I can hear people around me and I can hear God. I find that wonderful.

May I pray for you and me?

Lord Jesus, it's so wonderful that you have opened the door for us to have a conversation with God. We thank You for doing that for us. Help us to work at this communication. Help us to read the Bible, pray and listen. You have much to tell us. In Your name, Jesus. Amen.

Try writing your prayers, then try to listen to God talk to you. Record what you hear.

Journal Your Thoughts

It's Hard to Stop the Mental Racket When I Pray

Listening

The other day I read a post about being an active listener and how important it can be. I have a head that never stops thinking except when I am asleep. And I'm not sure about that either as I do have dreams.

When I'm listening to someone, I do try to keep eye contact and be fully engaged. The problem is that I can get so engaged with what has been said that it brings to mind other ideas. And then I feel like I'm going to burst because I want to interact. I know I need to wait for the person to stop talking or for a break in the conversation. But as you see this leads to not actively listening. If I wait until they are finished, I will lose those thoughts. That shouldn't bother me – but it does.

I want to work on this part of me.

I want to find a way of actively listening without interrupting.

While in church, I take sermon notes. This helps me to relax, assured that if I have a question, I can jot it down to ask the minister later.

This whole thing made me think about my relationship with God and how I talk to Him. My prayers consist mostly of my talking. Period. That's it.

But what if my prayers consisted of listening too?

Could I sit still and clear my mind of my thoughts and questions and wait for God to speak?

The first time I tried this, years ago, I couldn't sit still for longer than five minutes. After that time, I became restless and uncomfortable.

I have, over the years, become better at this. But lately, I know I have once again reverted to talk, talk and talk some more.

That is until one day when I read a verse in the Bible.

Psalm 32:8

> *I will instruct you and teach you in the way you should go; I will counsel you with my loving eye on you.*

Oh my – yes that's what's been missing I thought.

I need to STOP what I'm doing and go to God to hear Him.

He says He will instruct, teach and counsel me.

For the first time in a long time, I sat quietly before God.

It took me a few uncomfortable, head-filled restless minutes, but eventually, I relaxed and opened my heart and head to His Presence.

I felt Him. I felt the peace of Jesus. I visualized a few pictures in my mind too. But mostly I heard – You've come back.

In my SIMPLE Method of Bible study, the outline that uses the letters s,i,m,p,l and e, gives us a time to pray and listen to God.

May I pray for you and me?

Father, we know we have very active minds that sometimes don't want to shut down. Help us to learn how to clear our hearts and minds of the mental chatter and be able to hear from You. Give us time to be present with You. In Jesus' name. Amen.

While you study a verse or passage take time to pray and listen to God's voice.
You will be inspired.

Journal Your Thoughts

Five Ways to Learn how to Devote Yourself to Prayer

Colossians 4:2 says:

> *Devote yourselves to prayer, being watchful and thankful.*

I like that idea – to devote myself to prayer – but how can I accomplish it?

I needed help. One of the resources I found was Mark Batterson's Draw the Circle – The 40 Day Prayer Challenge.

While studying this book I realized that prayer is beyond any expectations that I ever thought possible. I loved it so much that I took a group through the study too.

I would like to become a watchman for God.

And to do that I must stay alert to what's happening around me. That way I can help others, I can thank God and be grateful for His help.

Mark says:

> *Prayer is the difference between seeing with our physical eyes and seeing with our spiritual eyes.* [ix]

Here are five ways I have found to bridge the gap between earth and the unseen world.

Be specific

Pray specifically for God to open your eyes. Only God can open our spiritual eyes.

I know when I do this that I will be seeing things I would normally pass over. I will see divine appointments. I will notice where God is leading me.

The Aramaic word for "prayer" (slotha) means "set a trap for". Instead of thinking of prayer as a list of wants we need to see prayer as a way to ask God to speak to us. Waiting for Him to give us wisdom. Waiting for Him to answer our questions.

Have a conversation with God

Prayer is a two-way conversation. We need to remember it isn't just us speaking. God can reply. God speaks through our dreams, our desires, our promptings, impressions and ideas. The Holy Spirit helps us to do this. We could say the Holy Spirit is our Sixth Sense. He helps us see into the spiritual realm and to hear across the divide between earth and heaven.

Work and practice

Be prepared for work and practice. Set a time each day to practice the art of prayer. Set your alarm, if you need to get up earlier. Be specific in what you ask and then wait. This prayer journey must become routine. We need to do it each day.

Read the Bible daily

Read God's Word daily. Start using it as an offence. It's a battle against Satan. Pray the Scriptures.

Mark Batterson says:

> *Quit talking to God about your problem and start telling your problems about God.* [x]

Change up your reading

Try reading devotionals, Bible studies along with your Bible.

This prayer journey can be exciting. But we need to begin. If you haven't asked God to open your spiritual eyes, do so today and begin a wonderful, exciting journey into communicating with God.

May I pray for you and me?

Thank You, Father, for this wonderful way to communicate with you. Help us to learn more and more as we ask for Your help. Jesus taught us how to pray by saying, "Our Father Who art in heaven, Hallowed be thy name. Thy kingdom come, thy will be done on earth as it is in heaven. Give us this day our daily bread and forgive us our trespasses as we forgive those who trespass against us. Lead us not into temptation but deliver us from evil. For thine is the kingdom and the power and the glory. For ever and ever. Amen." Thank You, Jesus.

Prayer is a journey.
Remember to take time each day to pray and read God's Word.

Journal Your Thoughts

How Our Amazing God Changes Our Newness

Coming up is the season for weddings in my country. It's not that weddings don't occur at other times of the year, but most of them are between May and September.

The usual dress worn by the bride is white. That reminded me of the words, "Pure spotless bride of Christ." That's the perfect union. And it will be one of purity.

Ephesians 5:27

> *He did this to present her to himself as a glorious church without a spot or wrinkle or any other blemish. Instead, she will be holy and without fault. (NLT)*

That does not always happen in our broken world.

Praise God we have a Saviour that can make us as white as snow right now.

Most of us know that when Jesus saves us all our sins are forgiven and we can come before God in our newness.

However, I think we forget that our newness can still be tainted by our brokenness and the world. We need to work on this every day.

Hebrews 12:10

> *While we were children, our parents did what seemed best to them. But God is doing what is best for us, training us to live God's holy best. (MSG)*

For us to be holy before God, He uses circumstances, thoughts, and His Word to teach us.

Ephesians 4:24 tells us:

> *Put on the new self, created to be like God in true righteousness and holiness,*

God teaches us through His Word. Daily reading of the Bible can reveal the truth to us that we either didn't know or buried deep.

Did I judge someone?
Am I critical?
Do I complain?
Did I forget to smile at the salesclerk?

2 Corinthians 7:1 tells us

> *to purify ourselves from everything that contaminates body and spirit, perfecting holiness out of reverence for God?*

Should I watch that movie?
Should I listen or partake in that gossip?

Should I eat a food that I know is bad for my health?

Praise God that He talks to us. We only need to listen and be aware of the lesson He teaches.

God is here.

He surrounds us.

As a child of God, our newness is ever-changing as He builds us into His likeness.

1 John 3:2-3 says,

> *But friends, that's exactly who we are: children of God. And that's only the beginning. Who knows how we'll end up! What we know is that when Christ is openly revealed, we'll see him—and in seeing him, become like him. All of us who look forward to his Coming stay ready, with the glistening purity of Jesus' life as a model for our own. (MSG)*

I struggle here on earth, but I press on towards that goal, by focusing on Christ and His Word.

May I pray for you and me?

Lord, it is a struggle for us to be like You. As we confess daily those thoughts and actions that did not reflect you, we accept your forgiveness and try again, and again. Thank You for Your Word that continues to reveal Your truth and more about ourselves. In Jesus' name. Amen.

What is God teaching you when you read the Bible?
Stay in the Word and learn.

Journal Your Thoughts

What's Under There?

While renovating our kitchen, built about 40 years ago, I was surprised to find things that were hidden under the cupboards. Things that would have devastated me if I knew they were there before.

I hate to tell you what I found. Besides the inevitable dirt and wood chips, there were also roach bodies. Yuck. And either mouse or roach excrement. Double yuck.

Also, while doing this renovation my husband decided we needed to take one of the walls right back to the studs to give him a firmer foundation to affix the cupboards.

As I cleaned up the mess with a heavy-duty vacuum, I thought about how this reflects our lives.

We keep many ugly things hidden away – sometimes not even knowing they're there. But when we uncover them, we need a strong vacuum to clean up the mess.

Jesus is our vacuum!

He can clean every mess we have in our lives if we let Him. He may need to go deep – right down to our studs to rebuild us the way He wants.

God already sees the mess – He knows what we have hidden away. God knows the sin in our hearts. Yes, I said sin because we all have it. We don't want to admit it, but we do.

As God chips away, like a sculptor, He is refining us. He is creating a being that will be ready to take a place in God's Kingdom.

Reading from **Psalm 66:10**,

> *For you, God, tested us;*
>
> *you refined us like silver.*

I love the saying, "God is not finished with me yet."

Philippians 1:6

> *There has never been the slightest doubt in my mind that the God who started this great work in you would keep at it and bring it to a flourishing finish on the very day Christ Jesus appears. (MSG)*

And that's a sure thing. Each day as I confess what it is in my heart, He hears me and accepts and forgives me.

I have a ways to go but I also know God is faithful to show me exactly what needs renovating in my life.

Now that we have a sturdy, new, clean kitchen it will be a reminder to me to seek out all the unseen messes under the surface of my life. I will ask Jesus to reveal those things to me.

I hope that you will do the same thing.
Ask to see what your messes are.
Ask for Jesus to help clean them up.

May I pray for you and me?

Father, we know many areas need renovation in our hearts and souls. Please help us to figure out what they are and work towards finishing the work so we can be pure in Your sight. In Jesus' name. Amen.

When you look at yourself, look deeply into who you are in Christ.
What needs to be fixed?
Read God's Word and He is sure to show you.

Journal Your Thoughts

Prayer Books

The Workbook of Living Prayer by Maxi Dunham
Too Busy Not to Pray by Bill Hybels
The Power of Persistent Prayer by Cindy Jacobs
Prayer of Jabez by Bruce Wilkinson
The Workbook of Living Prayer by Maxi Dunham

Devotional/Teaching Books/Resources

My Utmost for His Highest by Oswald Chambers
The Best of C.H. Spurgeon
Draw the Circle by Mark Batterson
psalms alive! by David Kitz
How to Be Filled with the Holy Spirit by A.W. Tozer
Refresh by Ron Hughes
One Thousand Gifts by Ann Voskamp
HopeStreamRadio – Growing Through God's Word

About the Author

Janis Cox has been writing online since 2008. A late bloomer for Christ, she started her writing journey in 2001 by writing poetry while journaling and reading her Bible. As God spoke to her and answered her questions, she realized how important it was to have this open communication with Him.

Challenged by Jesus, Janis started a new blog in 2012 the year she published *Tadeo Turtle* (an illustrated story for ages up to 6). By 2016 her second story ready, *The Kingdom of Thrim* (ages 5 and up) was published.

Janis joined *Hope Stream Radio, an Internet radio Station,* in 2016 and podcasted almost 150 programs for them.

Some of those podcasts have now become this book and are designed to bring hope for new Christians (and old ones too) to discover the power of God's Word.

Her Facebook group called *Growing Through God's Word* helps all Christians stay on track with their study of the Bible and prayer. Join the group.

If you enjoyed this compilation, stayed tuned for the next book in the series.

Note from the Author: Reviews are gold to authors! If you have enjoyed this book, would you consider reviewing it on Amazon.com? Thank you!
www.janiscox.com

---

[i] Mark Batterson, *Draw the Circle: The 40 Day Prayer Challenge* (Michigan: Zondervan, 2016, 75)

[ii] Batterson, 75-76

[iii] Batterson, 82

[iv] Holy Spirit" written and sung by Sally Meadows and Stan Garchinski, produced by Bart McKay Productions, Saskatoon.

[v] Oswald Chambers, *My Utmost for His Highest* (Michigan, Discover house Publications, 1992, Sept 2)

[vi] Chambers, June 6

[vii] Get Your Daily Dose of Wisdom." Updated. Accessed February 8, 2020. https://utmost.org/classic/work-out-what-god-works-in-classic/.

[viii] "Frederick W Faber." Daily Christian Quotes. Accessed February 14, 2020. https://www.dailychristianquote.com/frederick-w-faber-12/.

[ix] Mark Batterson, *Draw the Circle: The 40 Day Prayer* Challenge (Michigan: Zondervan, 2016, 67)

[x] Batterson, 88

www.ingramcontent.com/pod-product-compliance
Lightning Source LLC
Chambersburg PA
CBHW071518040426
42444CB00008B/1709